YOU CHOOSE
BOOKS

D0196839

PERSEUS THE HERO

AN INTERACTIVE MYTHOLOGICAL ADVENTURE

by Nadia Higgins
illustrated by Nadine Takvorian

Consultant: Dr. Laurel Bowman
Department of Greek and Roman Studies
University of Victoria
Victoria, BC, Canada

CAPSTONE PRESS
a capstone imprint

You Choose Books are published by Capstone Press,
1710 Roe Crest Drive, North Mankato, Minnesota 56003
www.mycapstone.com

Library of Congress Cataloging-in-Publication Data
Names: Higgins, Nadia, author.
Title: Perseus the hero : an interactive mythological adventure /
by Nadia Higgins.
Description: North Mankato, Minn. : Capstone Press, 2017. |
Series: You choose books. You choose ancient Greek myths | Includes
bibliographical references and index.

Identifiers: LCCN 2015044068
ISBN 9781491481127 (library binding)
ISBN 9781491481172 (pbk.)
ISBN 9781491481219 (ebook pdf)
Subjects: LCSH: Perseus (Greek mythology)—Juvenile literature.
Plot-your-own stories.
Classification: LCC BL820.P5 H54 2017 | DDC 398.20938/02--dc23
LC record available at http://lccn.loc.gov/2015044068

Editorial Credits
Michelle Hasselius, editor; Russell Griesmer, designer;
Wanda Winch, media researcher; Kathy McColley, production specialist

Image Credits
Shutterstock: Alex Novikov, scroll, Eky Studio, stone wall,
pandapaw, 102, reyhan, stone, Samira Dragonfly, gold frame,
Tymonko Galyna, Greek column

Printed and bound in Canada.
009632F16

Table of Contents

About Your Adventure

YOU are the mighty hero Perseus. You must go on an epic quest to save your mother and claim your throne as ruler of Argos. On your journey, you will face deadly monsters, cunning gods, and powerful kings. Can you survive?

Chapter One sets the scene. Then you choose which path to take. Follow the directions at the bottom of each page. The choices you make determine what happens next. After you finish your path, go back and read the others for more adventures.

YOU CHOOSE the path you take through this mythical adventure.

The Strings of Fate

Long ago, King Acrisius of Argos sought an oracle to learn about his future. The oracle foretold that the king would be killed by his daughter's son. Fearing the oracle's prediction, King Acrisius locked his daughter, Danae, in a bronze dungeon with no doors. There was just one slit of a window at the top to let in the sun.

Danae spent her days singing to her reflection in the mirror. The god Zeus heard her voice rising from the earth, and he fell in love. Zeus turned himself into golden slivers of light and shone down in Danae's chamber. That's when your story—the great story of Perseus—began.

Turn the page.

You had curls of gold as a baby, just like the god. Acrisius' heart almost stopped when he heard your infant cries coming from the dungeon. The next day, Acrisius locked you and your mother in an oak chest. Then he pushed the chest into the rough ocean waters. You and your mother could easily have drowned.

For days the chest bobbed and spun on the waves. Then one day the water stilled and sunlight streamed in the chest. You and your mother landed safely on the Greek island of Seriphus.

Years have passed, and now you are a young man living with your mother and the kindly fisherman, Dictys. But you are not a mere farmer or fisherman—you are a son of Zeus.

Your gray eyes hold a cleverness far beyond your years. You are stronger than three oxen combined. You are so daring, you dive off cliffs and chase sharks.

But all is not well for you on Seriphus. Dictys' brother Polydectes is king. The jealous ruler cannot bear to see Dictys happy. Though he rules Seriphus, Polydectes has always envied his brother. Polydectes sees your beautiful mother and decides she will be his queen.

"No, thank you," Danae said politely when Polydectes asked for her hand. He continued to ask, and Danae declined, each time more firmly. The king sent her gold bracelets, silk ribbons, fresh figs, and every other object a queen might desire. But no gift could woo her.

Turn the page.

You have warned Polydectes to stay away. It appears he took you seriously. The king has announced his plans to marry another maiden. But you remain wary. You worry Polydectes still intends to make your mother his bride.

To show his goodwill, the king has invited your family to the engagement feast. All the other guests have come with expensive gifts. But you have no gift to offer the king.

"But, Perseus," King Polydectes smiles. "You alone can bring me what I want most of all."

"What is it?" you ask. "Whatever it is, I will bring it, on my mother's honor."

"Bring me the head of Medusa, the Gorgon," Polydectes says.

The crowd gasps at the king's request. But you stand tall. Your life as Perseus the hero has begun. Choose the quest you wish to explore.

To accept Polydectes' challenge and find Medusa, turn to page 13.

To explore the seas as a great adventurer, turn to page 45.

To try to reclaim your throne from King Acrisius, turn to page 77.

CHAPTER 2

The Quest for Medusa's Head

You've accepted Polydectes' challenge to slay Medusa. And now it feels like a litter of snakes has hatched inside your gut.

The Greek elders have a saying—your blessing is your curse. You never really understood it until today. Your reputation for fearlessness is legendary throughout Seriphus. But today it may become your downfall.

Turn the page.

Medusa. When you boasted that you would bring back her head, the crowd was stunned. Your mother screamed, and King Polydectes smirked.

"Who—what—is Medusa?" you ask your mother back at your cottage. Her voice catches in her throat as she tells you the story.

"Medusa is a Gorgon, one of three sisters who live hidden in the deserts of Africa," your mother says. "Medusa is the only sister who can be killed. But it won't be easy. She has scaly green skin and poisonous snakes for hair. Some say she cries blood. And just one glance at Medusa's face will turn a man to stone."

You're speechless as you take it all in. Three fearsome Gorgons. Poisonous snakes for hair. A deadly gaze.

"This is your fate, Perseus," your mother sighs. "May the gods help you."

Your mother is right. You need help from the gods. But which god will you ask? Athena is the goddess of wisdom and protector of heroes. But Zeus is the king of the gods, as well as your father.

To ask for help from Athena, turn to page 16.

To ask for help from Zeus, turn to page 37.

You decide to ask Athena for help on your quest. As you walk into the goddess' temple, an owl flies in and lands on the rafters. The bird is Athena's symbol and pet.

"Perseus," a woman's voice echoes behind you. "Follow me."

You follow Athena's owl along the seashore. You travel to the mouth of a cave that smells like seaweed and saltwater. Three young women with hair down to their ankles come out from the darkness.

"Perseus, you've come at last!" they cry. "We are the Nymphs of the north. We have been expecting you. We have what you need."

One of the nymphs holds out two items.

"You must choose just one magical gift," she tells you. In one hand, she holds a pair of gold sandals with feathered wings. "Wear these sandals," she says, "and you will fly like a bird."

In her other hand is a gleaming wooden stick. "This is the staff of revival," she explains. "If you die, this staff will bring you back to life. But remember, its magic works only once."

The nymph closes her eyes and begins to sing.

"A magic item you must take. Choose well; make no mistake. One choice makes your way fair. The other only brings despair."

The three nymphs look at you expectantly. Which object will you choose?

To choose the staff, turn to page 18.

To choose the sandals, turn to page 20.

As soon as the staff is in your hand, the nymphs disappear. Their footprints have vanished. Their cave is just a dune of sand.

"Please, come back!" you call out. "Which way do I go?" But all you hear is the crashing of ocean waves.

You know there is no time to waste, so you begin your search for Medusa. Your mother told you the monster lives in the desert, so you turn inland. You carry the staff at your side. But without the winged sandals, you must walk. You walk for days. Your own regular sandals soon wear down to nothing. You continue on barefoot.

The weather gets hotter and hotter, and you're having trouble finding water. The sky is endless blue, without a cloud in sight. Your hands are full of sores from ripping open cactuses. You ate their juicy meat and drank the liquid inside. But now there are no cactuses left.

Eventually you die alone in the desert. As promised the staff of revival brings you back to life—but as a cactus. You live the rest of your days as a cactus in the sandy desert.

THE END

To follow another path, turn to page 11.

To learn more about Perseus, turn to page 103.

"You have chosen well," the second nymph says. "You may choose again."

She steps forward with two new objects. In her right hand is a brass helmet with red fringe across the top. It's dinged up and bent a little.

"This is the helmet of invisibility," she says. "It will make you invisible for one heroic task."

In the nymph's other hand is a cotton cloak that ties around the neck.

"Here is the cloak of friendship," she says. "It will make all living beings be kind to you."

The nymph hisses a plea. "Perseus, be careful. Be wise! One object is your reward, the other your demise!"

To choose the cloak, go to page 21.

To choose the helmet, turn to page 24.

You grab the cotton cloak, and the nymphs vanish. Every trace of them is gone. Ocean waves crash on the beach where their cave used to be.

You put on the winged sandals and float into the sky. It's so much fun, you laugh out loud.

Next you tie on the cloak of friendship and a warmth fills your heart. You don't know which way to go, but it doesn't seem to matter.

As you head along the shore, seagulls perch on your shoulders. Crabs crawl out of the water to tickle your toes. Fishermen bring you jugs of clam juice for your journey.

Turn the page.

As night falls you seek out shelter to rest. You come upon a cave where a Cyclops lives. Normally you would fear the one-eyed giant, but you know he won't eat you while you wear the cloak. Instead he picks you up lovingly in his giant hand. You fall asleep in his palm.

The next morning you wake up inside a cage. Your cage has a bed, a swing, a bowl of food, and a little stuffed toy. The Cyclops' huge smiling face appears in front of you. He sticks a finger through the bars and tickles your belly. The Cyclops loves you so much, he has decided to keep you as his pet forever.

THE END

To follow another path, turn to page 11.

To learn more about Perseus, turn to page 103.

The nymphs seem pleased with your choice.

Surely the gods must favor you!

"You must choose one final time," says the third nymph, offering you two more items.

The first is a simple pouch that closes with a string. "This is an endless pouch," the nymph says. "You may fill it with whatever you wish, and it will always stay the same size."

The second item is a wooden cup. It looks a little chewed around the rim. "And this is an endless cup," the nymph says. "It fills with water when you wish it. With this cup, you will never feel thirsty on your desert journey."

The nymph's piercing blue eyes look into your own. Which item will you choose?

To choose the pouch, go to page 25.

To choose the cup, turn to page 40.

"Well done!" Athena's voice rings. The nymphs have vanished, but Athena and her owl stand before you. The owl is perched on a shiny golden rectangle.

"This is my shield," Athena says. "Use it like a mirror to see Medusa's reflection. You will be safe from her deadly gaze."

THWACK! Something strikes the ground next to your foot. "My brother Hermes sends this gift," says Athena. "His sword can slice through the monster." The curved sword sticks out of the sand.

"Now you must seek the three Gray Sisters," Athena commands. "They will lead you to Medusa's desert lair. Follow my pet." And with that, Athena's owl flies away.

Turn the page.

You strap on the winged sandals and shove everything else into your endless pouch. You fly after the owl, amazed at how effortless it is to soar through the air on the winged sandals.

Soon Athena's owl swoops down on three old ladies sitting around a fire. Together they are weaving a gray blanket that covers their laps.

"Who's there?" one creaky voice calls out. She looks right at you, but she doesn't seem to see you. A single tooth hangs in her mouth. "Pass me the eye so I can see," she says to her sister.

"I will if you pass me back the tooth," her sister says.

You're not sure how to approach these strange women. You crouch behind a rock to hide.

You watch the Gray Sisters for several minutes. It seems they share just one eye and one tooth among the three of them. As they weave their blanket, the sisters take turns eating berries and looking at the sky.

Are these three old ladies friends or foes? You need important information from them. How will you get it?

To reason with the Gray Sisters, turn to page 28.

To steal the sisters' eye and tooth and blackmail them, turn to page 31.

"Excuse me, sisters," you say, using your best manners as you step into the witches' circle.

"Who dares to step between the Gray Sisters?" one of them hisses. She stares at you with the eyeball. In her hand, she points the tooth at you like a dagger.

"I don't mean to be rude," you try again. "I'm just wondering … I mean, would you mind telling me the way to Medusa's lair?"

"And what business do you have with our dear friend Medusa?" another witch asks, after grabbing the eye and popping it into her own head.

The three sisters are standing now. They form a circle around you. You don't need to say anything more.

"Look, sisters! He has the winged sandals of Hermes," the sister with the eye tells the others.

"We know who you are, Perseus!" another sister yells. "Sisters, attack!"

The old women are amazingly strong. Two of them pin you down, while the third tears you apart.

"Hey, save some for me!" one sister shouts. These are the last words you hear before you are eaten alive.

THE END

To follow another path, turn to page 11.

To learn more about Perseus, turn to page 103.

You fly over and swipe the eye and tooth from the women's wrinkled hands. The items feel cold and slimy. You have to force yourself not to drop them.

"Hello, ladies," you say as the sisters turn to the sound of your voice.

The sisters soon realize what you've done. "Thief!" the first sister cries.

"Give us back our eye and tooth!" screams the second. All three sisters reach for you blindly in the air.

"I will return your eye and tooth," you promise." As soon as you tell me the way to Medusa's lair."

Turn the page.

The Gray Sisters have no choice but to tell you what you want to know. "Follow the sound of the hissing snakes," the third sister says.

"Thanks for your help!" you call, as you throw the eye and tooth by the sisters' feet.

You fly toward a distant hiss. Soon you find yourself above the deserts of Africa. The hissing sound is almost a roar when you see three hunched figures down below. You recognize their green skin and snaky hair. These must be the Gorgon sisters.

Now is the time to use your helmet. As soon as you put it on, your reflection disappears from the shield. You fly backwards, holding your shield in front of your face.

In your shield, you watch as the sisters get closer and closer. You are safe from turning to stone as long as you only see them in the shield's reflection.

"I smell human," one of the sisters says. She swipes at the sky and just barely misses your shin.

It's time to strike. But which one is Medusa? You remember your mother's words. Of the three, only Medusa is mortal. The other two cannot be killed. You must choose carefully.

To attack the Gorgon with bloody tears dripping from her eyes, turn to page 35.

To attack the Gorgon with sharp, pointed tusks, turn to page 42.

Steady, steady, You whisper to yourself as you float over the Gorgon's head. Her snakes are snapping at your invisible elbows. You're not sure how to attack.

Then you remember your endless pouch. It will hold anything you put inside. You close your eyes and turn. You drop the pouch over the monster's head.

Thank the gods, you think, as you see the pouch cover the Gorgon's squirming snakes.

Then as fast as a tornado, you turn, sword arm raised. SLASH! You feel the blade cut cleanly through the monster's neck.

Turn the page.

As the Gorgon's head falls, you snatch the string of the pouch and fly away with the Gorgon's severed head. The slithering snakes on the monster's head go quiet and limp. They are dead—and so is Medusa. You attacked the right Gorgon.

The other Gorgon sisters quickly realize what you have done. They want revenge and rush to attack. You fly away on your winged sandals, narrowly escaping their deadly grasp.

Your heroic deed is done. The birds have already begun to spread news of your triumph. You return to Seriphus and King Polydectes with his gift.

THE END

To follow another path, turn to page 11.

To learn more about Perseus, turn to page 103.

You peer into Zeus' temple. It looks dark and cold inside. Giant statues guard the entrance. Did you see one of them twitch?

"Father?" you call. "It is I, Perseus. Can you help me in my quest?"

One of the giant statues in front of you comes forward. It's a stone replica of Zeus with a bulging chest and long beard. The statue is holding a lightning bolt, Zeus' signature weapon.

"Oh, thank you!" you say as you bow down at the statue's feet. You wait for your divine father to grant you the wisdom you need.

"Well hello, noble Perseus," the statue says.

Turn the page.

Something's wrong. The statue speaks in a woman's voice, not the voice of your father. Suddenly you realize it's Zeus' wife, Hera. You've heard the stories about the powerful goddess. She's insane with jealousy about Zeus' love affairs with human women. And she takes out her wrath on Zeus' half-human children.

You stand up to run, but it's too late. The stone thunderbolt starts to glow and crackle. A bright light blinds you. ZAP!

As the thunderbolt hits your chest, your last thought is of your mother. Your death will surely break her heart.

THE END

To follow another path, turn to page 11.

To learn more about Perseus, turn to page 103.

As soon as they hand you the cup, the nymphs disappear. You put on the sandals and do a somersault in the air. But this is no time to play.

It looks like you're going to have to find Medusa on your own. You fly through the deserts of Africa, filling your cup with water many times over.

After months of searching, you find Medusa. She is sleeping against a rock alone. Her face is turned down. The snakes that grow from her head are sleeping too. Surely the gods are protecting you!

You put on your helmet and float over to her, invisible. You grab Medusa's gruesome head with your bare hands and close your eyes. With a grunt you chop off the monster's hideous head before she wakes up.

You did it! The monster is dead. Still, you need to be careful. Even in death, Medusa's face will turn onlookers to stone. As you fly away, you turn the Gorgon's gaze away from you. You don't want to glance down at it by accident.

THWACK! THUD! CLANK! Suddenly it feels like someone is hitting you with stones. You look up and see stone birds are falling from above. The birds must have glanced into Medusa's dead eyes.

BAM! All of a sudden a large stone bird hits you on the head. You die instantly from the blow and fall to the ground. Even in death, your hand stays tangled in Medusa's snakes.

THE END

To follow another path, turn to page 11.

To learn more about Perseus, turn to page 103.

Looking at your target in your shield, you fly into position. You raise your sword. SLASH! You lop off the Gorgon's head with a single swing.

But you barely have time to savor your heroism. In the shield you see the head fly back onto the Gorgon's body. It wasn't Medusa! It was one of her immortal sisters.

Even if they can't see you, the deadly Gorgons know you're there. They swing their arms at the air around you.

Suddenly one of them catches your clothes with her claws. Three pairs of scaly hands pull you down to the ground.

Shutting your eyes, you swing blindly with your sword. But you can't keep up your strength. The Gorgons' snakes are biting up and down your arms and legs. Sharp fangs sting your belly, and you can feel blood pouring down your face.

Now your whole body feels heavy. You feel like a stone sinking to the bottom of the ocean.

Forgive me, Mother, you think. This is your last thought as the snakes' deadly poison reaches your brain.

THE END

To follow another path, turn to page 11.

To learn more about Perseus, turn to page 103.

CHAPTER 3

Monsters and Gods

"I am Perseus the hero, son of Zeus and slayer of Medusa," you say as you fly away from Medusa's lifeless body.

With the help of Athena, you were able to find Medusa and lop off her head with your sword. Now you carry Medusa's head with you. It is a deadly weapon. Just one gaze into Medusa's lifeless face turns onlookers to stone.

Turn the page.

The gods have given you gifts to help you on your quest. Hermes' winged sandals will let you float among the clouds. You also carry a magical pouch. You can fill it with whatever you like, and it will always stay the same size. You store Medusa's head inside the pouch as you travel.

Now you are eager to get back to Seriphus. You can't wait to see Polydectes' face when you return with the monster's head. Plus you are worried about your mother. You fear the king is still trying to force her to marry him.

As you fly away on your winged shoes, you look down on Medusa's body. A bright flash catches your eye and you stop, hovering in mid-air. Something white—pure white—is glowing from the neck of Medusa's bloody corpse. You move a little closer. It's a horse!

The winged horse Pegasus emerges from Medusa. Suddenly the majestic beast takes off into the air. One flap of his powerful wings sends streams of sand skittering across the ground underneath you. He looks like he's heading straight toward you. What's your next move?

To fly away on your winged sandals,
turn to page 48.

To ride Pegasus,
turn to page 61.

Pegasus is speeding your way. But is he coming at you? You're still far away, and you're not sure the horse sees you.

You fly up and out of the horse's path. WHOOSH-FLAP! WHOOSH-FLAP! WHOOSH-FLAP! Moments later Pegasus flies underneath you. You bob up and down in the wind. Then the air is still. The horse is off to some unknown destination.

You are safe. You fly toward Seriphus on your trusty sandals. You fly for days, until desert sands turn to ocean beaches. You savor the familiar smell of saltwater and the cries of seagulls. But now you hear a different kind of cry.

"Help! Please, help me!" a woman's voice calls to you from below.

Peering down you see a young woman chained to a boulder on the seashore. She is twisting and yanking at the shackles that pin her wrists. The ocean waves crash at her feet.

"My name is Andromeda. Please help me!" she calls out to you.

You land near Andromeda and try to help. You pull harder on the rings that hold Andromeda to the boulder, but they hold fast.

"Why are you chained here? What monster is coming?" you ask as you continue to pull.

Turn the page.

"My father the king left me here for the sea monster as a sacrifice to Poseidon," Andromeda says. "My mother made an enemy of Poseidon when she bragged that I was more beautiful than the mermaids. Poseidon has been punishing our kingdom ever since."

"Now please, hurry!" Andromeda begs. "The tide is coming in soon. The monster will be here any minute."

Andromeda begins to weep, but her sobs soon turn to screams. You feel a presence behind you. Turning, you see the sea monster rise out of the water. It looks like a giant octopus and a mammoth snake combined. It has several heads with fanged teeth and slurping tongues. Its powerful tentacles curl and snap in the air.

Thinking fast, you fly between the monster's heads and lure it away from the princess. That gives you a moment to think. In one hand is your sword. In the other is your magical pouch with Medusa's severed head. How will you attack?

To use your sword to try to kill the sea monster,
turn to page 53.

To use Medusa's head to turn the sea monster to stone,
turn to page 65.

One of the monster's giant tentacles curls around your waist and starts to squeeze. Breathless, you take your sword and stab into the sea monster's scaly flesh. It releases you. Then the monster comes at you with all its heads snapping.

You fly in and out of the whipping tentacles and wait for the right opportunity. And there it is! You see one head move away from the rest. You zip past it. It follows you like a dog chasing a ball. Then you cut back at the last second.

The monster is confused, and its head pauses in mid-air. You raise your sword with two hands and slice through the monster's neck with one clean cut. All the monster's tentacles go limp. Its body crumples into the ocean with a splash.

Turn the page.

After the monster's death, Andromeda's iron rings magically spring open. She leaps toward you with open arms.

"You saved me!" Andromeda says. "What's your name, hero?" she asks.

"Perseus," you tell her.

She kneels in front of you. "Perseus, I am forever in your debt. Will you marry me?"

To marry Andromeda,
go to page 55.

To continue on your quest alone,
turn to page 67.

The fates have led you on some strange journeys. First to Medusa, then to the sea monster, and now this: love!

You and Andromeda decide to get married the very next day. Andromeda's father feels terrible about what he has done to his daughter. He throws a luxurious feast in your honor. The tables are laden with scallops, artichokes, honey cakes, and other treats. Jugglers, acrobats, and musicians parade through the hall.

You and Andromeda are ready to take your vows when the room suddenly goes quiet. A band of armed men stands in the doorway.

"Stop this unlawful wedding!" their leader shouts. His hair bobs up and down with each word. "Andromeda is already engaged to me."

Turn the page.

"Phineas," Andromeda says. "Where were you when I was left for the monster? I'd be dead if it weren't for my true love, Perseus."

Phineas winces at Andromeda's words. Then he turns to you with a toothy smile. "Perseus," he croons. "Let's be reasonable. You just met Andromeda yesterday. You don't want to displease the gods by taking what belongs to another man. I beg you to leave. For your trouble, I offer you this bag of gold."

Phineas holds up a hefty bag. It clinks with coins. There must be enough gold in there to build a house for your mother and buy a new fishing boat for Dictys.

To take the money and continue on your journey, go to page 57.

To stay and marry Andromeda, turn to page 70.

You choose Phineas' gold over your love for Andromeda. As soon as the gold is in your hands, you feel strange. Your heart is racing. You're hot and incredibly itchy.

"What is happening?" you cry out. Your voice is soft, high, and squeaky.

Squeaky? You look down at your arms. They're covered in fur. Your hands are tiny paws. You're sitting on something that feels like rope. It's a tail! You have been turned into a mouse!

"What dishonorable conduct for a hero!" yells a mighty voice. It's the goddess Athena with her owl, her favorite pet.

Turn the page.

Athena's owl is staring at you. That's when it hits you. Owls eat mice!

"Ah!" you try to scream. But all that comes out is a squeak. You run away, but Athena's owl flies after you at top speed. Suddenly it catches you by the tail with its razor-sharp beak. The owl swallows you whole.

THE END

To follow another path, turn to page 11.

To learn more about Perseus, turn to page 103.

Hovering in the air, you crouch down and wait for Pegasus to reach you. As the wings pass over your head, you spring up. You grab the horse's mane and swing onto his broad back. Pegasus rears back and comes to a standstill. The horse looks at you, but his teeth are not bared.

"Fly to Seriphus," you command. Pegasus carries you off into the endless blue sky.

You travel for days. One evening you notice the sky looks tilted. The birds seem spooked, and they flap in dizzy circles around you.

"Whoa," you tell Pegasus. You land on the desert sand to get a better look.

"Oh, thank the gods!" a voice booms from behind you. "Perseus, hello! The birds told me you were flying by."

Turn the page.

A huge man is standing on a sand dune. His white beard grows well below his belly, and his toga is in tatters. The man is bent forward with his arms outstretched. The evening sky rests across his back.

You've heard of this man. He is Atlas, one of the mighty Titans. The Titans were the gods who came before Zeus and the other gods on Mount Olympus. Long ago the Titans lost an epic battle against the Olympic gods. Atlas' punishment is to hold up the sky forever.

"Hero, I have a favor to ask of you. It is worthy of your strength and courage," Atlas says, smiling. "My neck aches, and I need to stretch it. Would you mind holding the sky for me, just for a minute?"

To refuse Atlas' request, turn to page 64.

To give Atlas a break, turn to page 70.

Atlas' eyes narrow into slits. "What kind of hero are you?" he taunts. "You are Perseus, son of Zeus? But you won't help a tired old man for just one minute. Ha! Act like a hero, if you are one!" As he kicks sand at you with one foot, the sky practically topples on your head.

"Take it easy," you say. You push the sky back on straight. "Get a hold of yourself."

"Be gone, stranger!" Atlas says. "I thought I was in the presence of a hero. Obviously I was mistaken. Go away and let me be. I'm waiting for the great Perseus to help me."

To give Atlas a break, turn to page 70.

To prove that you are Perseus, turn to page 72.

To fly away, turn to page 73.

Andromeda is behind the monster, watching you. "Andromeda!" you shout. "Shut your eyes!"

You start to look behind you to make sure she heard you. But in the next instant, a tentacle slams you from the side. You go swirling off into the air. Another tentacle is coming at you from the other side.

You grab Medusa's head from your pouch and raise it to the monster. The tentacle is just inches from your face when it freezes. Its flesh changes from green to white as the monster turns to stone. Then all at once, everything is quiet—too quiet.

Turn the page.

Andromeda! You look back at the boulder. She is leaning forward, as if still pulling at her iron rings. Her mouth is open in a scream. But she is frozen in stone.

The sight of Andromeda feels like a punch to the gut. Grief stricken, you drop Medusa's head into the ocean. You land near Andromeda's statue and take off your winged sandals. You don't deserve gifts from the gods. You can't face your mother now. You spend the rest of your days wandering the earth, heartbroken.

THE END

To follow another path, turn to page 11.

To learn more about Perseus, turn to page 103.

"Andromeda, you are beautiful," you begin. Your face feels hot as you speak. "But you see, I can't … " you mutter. This is much harder than slaying a monster. "I … I'm sorry."

Andromeda smiles. "It's all right, Perseus. I understand. I am forever in your debt for saving me from that monster."

You walk with Andromeda back to her palace. Along the way you tell her about King Polydectes and your quest. Andromeda wishes you well and sends you on your way with a heavy bag of gold.

Turn to page 73.

Phineas' fake smile makes you suspicious. You'd never leave Andromeda with this man.

"Walk away now, Phineas," you command, "and nobody gets hurt."

"We'll see about that," Phineas says with a laugh. "Attack!" he commands his men.

Phineas' army is bigger than you thought. A band of 40 men storms into the room swinging their swords. The hall fills with screams as the wedding guests try to flee.

Phineas grabs Andromeda and holds a dagger to her throat. "Be on your way, Perseus," he snarls. "Or neither of us will marry the princess."

You plunge your hand into the magical pouch and clutch the limp snakes of Medusa's hair.

"Andromeda, close your eyes," you order as you hold up Medusa's head.

For a second, Phineas gasps. Then his gaping mouth freezes onto his stone face. After that, Phineas' men panic. They run away with their eyes closed, screaming and bumping into walls.

Carefully you shove Medusa's head back into the pouch. Then you put one winged sandal on your foot and hand the other to Andromeda. The two of you fly off to Seriphus.

Turn to page 73.

You know what it feels like to have a heavy responsibility. After all you are a hero now. That is part of the job.

"Okay," you say to Atlas. "Just for a minute."

"Oh, thank you! Thank you, Perseus!" Atlas exclaims.

Atlas shows you how to hold your arms out. Then he carefully rolls the sky onto your shoulders. It's so heavy, your knees almost buckle from the weight.

"Ah," Atlas sighs and stretches his neck. It cracks like fireworks.

"Almost done?" you ask. Beads of sweat are stinging your eyes.

But Atlas is walking away, his shoulders moving up and down. Wait a minute. Is he laughing?

"So long, fool!" Atlas says as he mounts Pegasus.

"No! Please!" you scream. "Don't leave me here. My mother needs me. I ..."

But it's no use. Atlas and Pegasus are halfway across the sky. Atlas tricked you into holding up the heavens forever.

THE END

To follow another path, turn to page 11.

To learn more about Perseus, turn to page 103.

You didn't leave your family and risk your life to be disrespected by some old fool.

"I am Perseus," you shout at Atlas. "And I can prove it."

You angrily shove your hand into your pouch and grab Medusa's head. You hold up Medusa's severed head to the Titan. Atlas smiles at the sight of the Gorgon's head. His grin is captured forever as he turns to stone.

You realize this is what Atlas wanted all along. Finally his burden has been taken from him. As sand settles on his shoulders, the Titan grows into the Atlas Mountains. You carefully return Medusa's head to your pouch.

"Farewell, Atlas," you say, as you and Pegasus continue on your way.

As you fly home, you take in all you see—fuzzy cattails, colorful fishing boats, and rocky cliffs. The familiar sights of home fill your heart with joy. As you touch down in Seriphus, the villagers run to meet you. Even as they greet you, you sense that something is wrong.

"King Polydectes is forcing your mother to marry him," one of the elders explains. "The king is hosting their wedding feast this very moment."

Without a word, you head straight to Polydectes' palace. You kick the banquet hall doors open and see a lavish wedding feast. Gold plates are next to lace tablecloths. Your mother is seated at the front of the table in a long ruffled wedding dress. Armed guards line the walls.

"Perseus!" your mother cries when she sees you. "Oh, my boy! You're alive!"

Turn the page.

Your mother stands to run toward you but is yanked back. You see that her feet are chained to her wedding throne. Hot rage burns inside your chest.

"Close your eyes, Mother," you warn.

As King Polydectes and his guards come at you, you grab Medusa's head from your pouch and wave it in their faces. Just like that, the guards and King Polydectes turn to stone.

You have fulfilled your promise to King Polydectes—although not quite in the way that he'd expected.

The people of Seriphus beg you to become their king, but you have a better idea. King Dictys will reign with Queen Danae at his side.

THE END

To follow another path, turn to page 11.

To learn more about Perseus, turn to page 103.

CHAPTER 4

Claim Your Throne

"Perseus! Over here! Look at me!"

When you walk down the streets of your birthplace, people call out your name. They pull at your toga or try to touch your golden hair. Some girls faint and land on the path ahead of you.

You are Perseus the hero. In the past several months, you have endured many adventures. You have battled the monster Medusa and lopped off her head. You have killed a giant sea monster. You have rescued your mother from the evil King Polydectes.

Turn the page.

Still, one unsettled matter still nags at your heart—your grandfather, King Acrisius. You were a baby when you saw him last. But you haven't forgotten how he locked you and your mother in an oak chest. He expected you to die in the ocean, no doubt.

For years your mother has urged you to claim your throne as the rightful heir of Argos. She's right. It's time. You've spent these past few weeks thinking of your approach. You've finally come up with a plan.

To go to Argos and face King Acrisius alone,
go to page 79.

To raise an army and attack Argos,
turn to page 85.

You love your fans, but it's a relief to be alone on the open road. As you walk along a sandy path, you stop to rest in a field of swaying wildflowers.

You are watching clouds drift overhead when a frail old man wobbles up to you. He looks unsteady as he leans on his staff. He points to the sign around his neck. Fortunes told for a modest fee.

You smile kindly at this foolish old man, but he looks you sharply in the eye.

"Heed me, Perseus," the old man says. "I have news of your grandfather, King Acrisius."

Turn the page.

The old man's words get your attention. How could this stranger possibly know about your grandfather?

"I am an oracle. I can see things," the old man says, as if reading your thoughts. "Pay now to learn your fate." He holds out his hand for a gold coin.

To learn your fate, turn to page 82.

To seek your own destiny, turn to page 90.

The oracle's fingers curl around your coin. Then he sits on the ground, folding his legs in front of him. He closes his eyes and remains still for several minutes. When he talks, his voice is young and strong.

"Perseus, believe my words however strange they be," the oracle begins. "Your grandfather holds you in great fear and with good reason. Your fates are twined like vines on a trellis. Acrisius learned this long ago. You will bring his end, he knows. It is fated so."

"I will kill my grandfather? How can that be?" you ask. You carry no weapons on your journey. You don't even have a knife to peel a lemon. "I won't do it!" you insist. "You're wrong!" But you feel uneasiness in your heart.

The oracle slowly stands up. He leans on his staff, looking at you blankly.

"Farewell, friend," he says, and he wanders off into the meadow. What will you do with the oracle's news?

To face your fate and continue to Argos,
turn to page 84.

To change your mind and go back to Seriphus,
turn to page 90.

Walking makes you feel better. The sounds of the meadow soothe you. You look up. The sun is high and bright. But as you continue down the path, something feels wrong. The birds seem to fly in aimless circles. The meadow's creatures scurry to their nests and burrows. Your shadow is growing quickly—too quickly—in front of you. The day feels like night.

A black circle covers the sun like a lid over a hole. A soft ring of light surrounds the black circle, and it glows from behind. It's a solar eclipse. The moon has blocked the sun.

You have heard of this event. Many Greek elders believe a solar eclipse is a bad omen. Could this be a sign of coming disaster?

To heed the warning and head away from Argos, turn to page 90.

To continue to Argos, turn to page 98.

Attention Greek warriors, young and old!

Join Perseus the hero in his quest.

March with him to Argos,

to reclaim his rightful throne!

You post flyers around Seriphus to recruit your army. Word spreads fast. By morning eager men are lining the street outside your door. You have nothing to pay them with except the promise of glory.

Your soldiers are the fishermen of Seriphus. Their backs are strong from throwing nets and rowing boats. They are practiced at spear throwing and with the bow and arrow. For weeks you and your army march steadily to your birthplace. You make an impressive sight as you arrive in Argos.

Turn the page.

"King Acrisius!" you shout. "Come out, you coward! Explain yourself!"

But you see that things are not right here. The fields are brown and the streets are empty.

A boy in a dirty tunic peers at you from behind a chipped statue. You approach him kindly, offering him a crust of bread from your purse.

"Where is the king of this land?" you ask.

"The king is nowhere to be found. He fled because Perseus is coming," the boy says. "The kingdom has fallen, and the people are starving."

"Do not fear Perseus, child," you tell the boy. "I am Perseus. I will set things right."

To continue to search for King Acrisius, go to page 87.

To stay and rebuild the kingdom, turn to page 100.

You promise the boy he will not be hungry when you are king. But right now you have other business to turn to.

"Onward!" you command your army.

You ask many along the road about the king, but no one knows where he is. You continue north for days, then turn west. Your soldiers are getting tired.

"Let's rest," you tell them as you head into a town along a river.

Your men are eager to soak their tired feet. While they sit by the river, you head to town to buy a goat. You're going to surprise them with some meat for dinner.

Turn the page.

You find a butcher shop in town. You push through its heavy doors. Then you stop in your tracks at the sound of your name. The butcher is crying. He's on his knees in prayer.

"Dear Zeus," the man whimpers. "Spare me the wrath of my grandson, Perseus. I will grant you any sacrifice!"

Now you know who this old man is. It is King Acrisius, disguised as a butcher! You leap forward.

"You already sacrificed me and my mother long ago!" you shout.

"Perseus!" the man cries. "The oracle predicted you would deliver my death. In fear I acted shamefully. I have dreaded this day, and I have longed for it. Please forgive me. You are the rightful king of this land. Claim your throne, and let's live in peace together."

To refuse Acrisius' request,
turn to page 96.

To grant Acrisius forgiveness and return to Argos as its king, turn to page 100.

You see a group of young men running toward you down the path. Their movements are easy and joyful, and it looks as though they are enjoying the day. It makes you smile to watch them. They point at you from the distance, and some start clapping.

"Perseus! Perseus the hero!" they call, running toward you. They recognized you by your golden curls, you learn later.

"Hello, friends!" you say, raising a hand to greet them. "Where are you heading?"

They explain that they are runners. They are on their way to an athletic competition in Thessaly.

"Join us, Perseus!" they say. They tempt you even more by telling you that your favorite event, discus, is part of the competition.

You gratefully accept. It's been a long time since you've had some fun. The idea of taking a day off to relax sounds great.

The games are in full swing as you head into the arena at Thessaly. The athletes at the games have their fans—but so do you.

"Perseus! Perseus!" the crowd chants, rising to its feet. People in the stands try to get your attention. Your new friends raise you up on their shoulders and carry you to the center of the field. The men ask you to compete.

Turn the page.

"Why not?" you say modestly as you head toward the discus throw.

Your clay discus has been sitting in the sun. It's warm in your hand as you walk to the competition area. You take your place and wait for your turn.

One, two, three, go! You push off with your legs, spinning to build your momentum. Your arms are out as you turn. The roaring crowd is a blur of colorful dots.

As you get ready to release the discus, something pinches your foot. It feels like a shell or a piece of broken discus. You flinch, and your foot twists. As you try to steady yourself, the discus slips from your hand.

Turn the page.

Your discus zings toward the crowd at lightning speed. You watch as if it is going in slow motion. You are frozen in shock as the runaway discus strikes an old man in the stands. He falls down like a knocked pin.

"He's dead!" a woman shouts as you cross the arena.

You run to the man's side. You stare into his lifeless grey eyes. It feels like spiders are crawling up and down your spine, and you realize that the man looks familiar.

"That's Acrisius, the king of Argos!" a man in the crowd says.

You may be a hero, but you are not above the laws of fate. The oracle's prediction has come true. You have killed your grandfather. The realization sinks into your heart and weighs heavy inside your chest.

Argos holds too much sorrow for you now. You bid farewell and resume your travels. What does your future hold now? Only the fates know.

THE END

To follow another path, turn to page 11.

To learn more about Perseus, turn to page 103.

You can't feel pity for this old man. What he did to you and your poor mother is unforgiveable.

"You jailed my mother like an animal!" you roar. "You broke her heart with loneliness. Then you sent us both to die."

You kill Acrisius in a moment of rage. You have fulfilled the oracle's prediction. Justice has been served.

But your father, Zeus, is disappointed in your actions. You could not control your anger, and you killed a man far weaker than you.

As punishment Zeus fills your heart with endless regret. It feels like hundreds of stones are tied around your neck. You can never face your army or your loved ones again.

With great sadness you wander off alone into Greece's wilderness. You spend the rest of your days living as a hermit on Mount Athos.

THE END

To follow another path, turn to page 11.

To learn more about Perseus, turn to page 103.

A few moments later, the sun shines brightly again. As your pounding heart stills, an eagle swoops down and hovers in front of you.

"You have made me proud, my son." The eagle speaks without moving its beak.

You are held spellbound as Zeus addresses you for the first time. "You have passed every test," Zeus says. "And now you have shown the greatest courage by standing up to fate itself. Continue to Argos. I have prepared the way."

A few days later, you arrive at the edge of a hill. You look down upon the kingdom of your birth. The fields are green. The houses gleam like a string of pearls along the river. Children with round faces chase each other through the meadow.

As you walk into Argos, the people greet you. They lead you to the town square, where a feast has been set up in your honor.

"An oracle told us to expect you," a woman says. "King Acrisius fled when he heard you were coming. King Perseus, we welcome you as our rightful ruler."

You prove to be a wise and compassionate king. You have big plans for Argos. You hire a team of scribes to record your heroic deeds. You erect a library to store the scribes' works. By your order every child, rich or poor, shall learn to read and write. You make sure your story will be passed on for generations.

Turn the page.

"Long live King Perseus!" the people of Argos shout as you walk the streets of your prosperous kingdom.

Because of your great justice, the strings of fate are cut. You are spared the grief of killing your grandfather, King Acrisius.

THE END

To follow another path, turn to page 11.

To learn more about Perseus, turn to page 103.

CHAPTER 5

A Classic Greek Hero

After Perseus slayed Medusa and defeated King Polydectes, he traveled to Athena's temple to give thanks. Perseus had used the Gorgon's head to turn hundreds of men to stone. He was weary from so much death. He offered Medusa's head to Athena for safekeeping.

Athena emblazoned a picture of Medusa's head on her shield. This struck fear in her enemies' hearts. Today hundreds of images of Athena and her famous shield are found in museums around the world.

Turn the page.

After his great adventures, Perseus settled down as the wise ruler of a peaceful kingdom. He and Queen Andromeda lived to a ripe old age and had many children. One of their descendants was the hero Heracles, who faced even more trials than Perseus.

After their long and happy life together ended, Athena placed Perseus and Andromeda among the stars. Their constellations still shine in the northern skies.

The Perseus myth has been retold countless times. The myth is still inspiring writers today. In the bestselling book series Percy Jackson, the main character Percy is based on Perseus. These new stories of Perseus add different twists to the old myth.

The story of Perseus is one of the first Greek myths. Why did it last so long? And why did it survive when so many other Greek myths were lost?

The Perseus myth holds all the elements of a great hero story. Perseus shouldn't have survived his many challenges. But he does, often thanks to help from the gods. They provide magical gifts, such as the flying sandals and the helmet of invisibility. And there's Perseus himself. He shows many admirable traits. His loyalty to his mother is what sets King Polydectes against him. Perseus is strong. But more than that, he is clever.

This beloved myth shows that heroes can win, and that the gods are on their side. It's a hopeful tale. No doubt, it will continue to hold people spellbound through the ages.

Greek Gods
and Goddesses

Athena—the goddess of wisdom and courage. Athena is Zeus' favorite child. She was born as a full-grown goddess from his forehead. Athena was one of the most beloved gods in ancient Greece. The Greek city of Athens is named after her.

Atlas—one of the twelve original Greek gods, known as Titans. As a Titan, Atlas waged war against Zeus and his gods, known as the Olympians. When Atlas lost, Zeus punished Atlas. Zeus forced Atlas to stand on the edge of Earth and hold up the sky until the end of time.

Hera—Zeus' wife and the goddess of marriage. Hera is best known for her intense jealousy. She is constantly tormenting Zeus' lovers and his half-mortal children.

Hermes—the messenger of the gods and Zeus' son. Hermes flies through the heavens and Earth on winged sandals, which he loans to Perseus for the hero's adventure. One of Hermes' most important jobs is to guide the souls of the dead to the Underworld.

Poseidon—the god of the seas and Zeus' brother. Poseidon is known for his temper. He is often shown holding a trident. When he gets mad, Poseidon slams his trident on the ground, causing an earthquake.

Zeus—the king of the gods, and the god of the sky and thunder. Zeus can be wise and kind, or cruel and violent. He has many famous love affairs with both goddesses and women. Zeus' symbol is a lightning bolt.

OTHER PATHS TO EXPLORE

In this book, you've experienced three adventures of Perseus the hero, but the story isn't over. Here are some other Greek myths that share characters with the stories you just read.

1. Heracles was one of Perseus' descendants. In one of his adventures, Hercules needs to retrieve three golden apples from a garden guarded by magical nymphs. He persuades Atlas to fetch them for him. In exchange, Heracles holds up the sky while Atlas is gone. Atlas returns with the apples, but he refuses to take back the sky. Heracles tricks Atlas to resume his duty. How is Heracles' adventure with Atlas similar to Perseus' interaction with Atlas? How is it different? (Integration of Knowledge and Ideas)

2. Perseus rides Pegasus in one of his adventures. But Pegasus is in many Greek myths. In one story, the hero Bellerophon rides Pegasus into battle against a chimaera. The fire-breathing chimaera is part lion, dragon, and goat. Pegasus flies above the monster while Bellerophon hurls lumps of lead into the chimaera's mouth. The monster's breath melts the lead, which runs down its throat and kills it. Greek mythology is full of mythological creatures. Can you invent one of your own? What's the creature's special power? What is its weakness? (Integration of Knowledge and Ideas)

3. Hera is Zeus' jealous wife. She hates all of Zeus' half-human children, including Perseus and Heracles. Hera is seen as an enemy to many of these heroes in Greek mythology. Hera is a powerful god with incredible strength. She is also the goddess of marriage and women, and she could bless or curse marriages. Using her powers, think of a way Hera could hurt Perseus after his quest. (Integration of Knowledge and Ideas)

GLOSSARY

constellation (kahn-stuh-LAY-shuhn)—a group of starts in the sky that seem to trace the outline of a person, animal or object

Cyclops (SY-klahpz)—a one-eyed giant

descendant (di-SEN-duhnt)—a person who can trace his or her family roots back to one person

discus (DIS-kuhss)—a large, heavy disk that is thrown in a track-and-field event

Gorgon (GOR-gehn)—a snake-haired monster in Greek mythology whose appearance can turn a human to stone

heir (AIR)—someone who has the legal right to receive the property or title of someone who has died

hermit (HUR-mit)—someone who lives alone and is isolated from other people

immortal (i-MOR-tuhl)—able to live forever

mermaid (MUR-mayd)—a sea creature with the upper body of a woman and the tail of a fish

nymph (NIMF)—a beautiful female spirit or goddess from Greek and Roman mythology who lived in a forest, meadow, mountain, or stream

omen (OM-uhn)—a sign of something that will happen in the future

oracle (OR-uh-kuhl)—a place or person a god speaks through; in myths, gods used oracles to predict the future or to tell people how to solve problems

temple (TEM-puhl)—a building used for worship

trident (TRY-dent)—a long spear with three sharp points at its end

READ MORE

Hoena, Blake A., and Daniel Ferran. *Perseus and Medusa: A Graphic Novel*. Graphic Revolve. North Mankato, Minn.: Stone Arch Books, 2014.

Weakland, Mark. *The Adventures of Perseus: A Graphic Retelling*. Ancient Myths. North Mankato, Minn.: Capstone Press, 2015.

Weiss, Lynne. *Perseus and Medusa*. Greek Heroes. New York: PowerKids Press, 2014.

INTERNET SITES

FactHound offers a safe, fun way to find Internet sites related to this book. All of the sites on FactHound have been researched by our staff.

Here's all you do:
Visit *www.facthound.com*
Type in this code: 9781491481127

BIBLIOGRAPHY

Barnett, Mary. *Gods and Myths of Ancient Greece*. New York: Smithmark Publishers, 1996.

Buxton, Richard. *The Complete World of Greek Mythology*. London: Thames & Hudson, Ltd., 2004.

Freeman, Philip. *Oh My Gods: A Modern Retelling of Greek and Roman Myths*. New York: Simon & Schuster, 2012.

Moncrieff, A. R. Hope. *Myths and Legends of Ancient Greece*. New York: Gramercy Books, 1995.

Ovid (trans. Mary M. Innes). *Metamorphoses*. New York: Penguin Books, 1955.

Stapleton, Michael. *The Illustrated Dictionary of Greek and Roman Mythology*. New York: Peter Bedrick Books, 1986.

Waterfield, Robin. *The Greek Myths: Stories of the Greek Gods and Heroes Vividly Retold*. New York: Metro Books, 2011.

Watts, Christopher, "Why Did the Greeks Tell Myths?" academia.edu, 2010, http://www.academia.edu/2922375/Why_did_the_Greeks_tell_Myths_Perseus (April 4, 2015).